Blockchain for Kids, Teens, Adults, and Dummies

Introduction to Crypto Investing and Blockchain Technology in Simple Words

Sweet Smart Books

Table of Contents

Introduction

Help! I want to know about cryptocurrency, but the moment I try to dive in deeply, it gets messy. It gets technical. It gets complicated. It's just one complication after the other. The articles are so full of technical terms they can leave you dizzy and spinning trying to figure out left from right.

I am here to help! Regardless of who you are, Bitcoin, crypto, and altcoins all play a dazzling role now and in the future. Just like cash and money have all become digital, crypto has practically become a possible form of payments and perhaps even investments.

But say, you know nothing about trading either? Investing? The whole lot? Even that gets over complicated sometimes, leaving people shaking their heads. It feels like they have skipped out on some subject in school or need to attend a whole four-year university to understand the foundation and basics of the online financial world.

Again, I am here to help! I believe that cryptocurrency and investing are oftentimes overcomplicated, and explained by people who forget at times that other people do not have prior knowledge of the trade. It comes to a point where you have to look up every second sentence and every second word to fully grasp what is going on.

The financial world might even seem boring for others, but they do want to partake in it to start growing another form of passive income. Investments are incredibly important in this day and age where the economy keeps struggling and people need to find ways to earn just a little bit more money.

On the other hand, it is best to learn and adapt to what the future may hold, and cryptocurrency, blockchain, and NFTs. It may become a part of your future, whether or not you were planning to invest in the first place.

Either way, here is a guide for kids, teens, adults, and dummies, anyone who has a great interest in understanding both blockchains and investing in crypto in a way that can be understood! So hold onto your seatbelts, by the time you arrive you will have a proper understanding of it all. You can show your knowledge to your friends, perhaps start dabbling in trading and investing, as well as finally understand what the news headlines are referring to. It is a win-win!

Chapter 1: How Does Money Work?

So let us start at the very beginning. Do you remember where the money comes from and how it works? If so, maybe it is still a good idea to brush up on your history. Not a lot of people make enough effort to understand how money works, just because it may already be deeply involved in our lives.

Money surrounds society. Without it, you really cannot get anywhere fast. So why is it that so few people know as much about money as they should? If you want to, go ask around and see how many people understand how money and currencies work.

You may see the blank stares as they realize that they perhaps don't know as much, or they give overcomplicated answers to avoid the fact that they simply don't know. Others may shrug their shoulders and smile, but some you might get a proper answer from. Either way, cryptocurrency and money run hand in hand, and it is best to start with the origin of the very thing which runs our economy.

History of Money

People did not naturally start exchanging with paper and coins. Instead, people used to barter their goods and services. What is bartering? Imagine you are a baker, and you would like some eggs. You barter three loaves of bread for a dozen eggs from the lady next door. That would be bartering, where you exchange a good or service you can do for another good or service another person can do.

But there is a big flaw with this system. Imagine you work with cattle, for example, and you would like some eggs now. You can't just hand over a whole cow for a dozen eggs. And even if you were going to use the meat of the cow, it won't last long, thus splitting pieces up is very impractical.

Therefore people came up with a system. They would use certain objects such as shells, amber, beads, silver, or gold with which to trade on. It worked as a basic form of currency.

The very first form of currency had been known as the Mesopotamian shekel, which had arisen almost 5,000 years ago. The earliest minted coins would have been from 650 to 600 BC with the Lydia and Ionia elites using stamped silver and gold to be able to pay for the armies.

As years passed by, silver, gold, lead, and copper were very common metals used in coinage throughout Asia, Europe, and North Africa. It was largely successful and popular due to its durability and the political leaders had greater control over the stamped coins (thus had greater chances of increasing their wealth). Money was used as a form of political control, wherewith their treasures they could raise armies, etc. They used to get gold and wealth by implementing taxes.

So, even many hundreds to thousands of years ago, taxes, unfortunately, have existed for the means to fund the government. And during history, the money itself acted as a form of record for various transactions as well as interactions.

Understanding Currency

Currency affects our everyday lives more than what you might ever imagine. Each time you swipe a card or pay for something in cash, you're making use of a currency. Currency is the money and perhaps what you could call the heart of an economy. It is what keeps businesses going, what gets warm food on your table, and a nice bed to sleep in.

Currency is a reference to actual money or the coins that are currently being used in a country. Of course, if you were to count, there would be a limited amount of money in each different country, but a lot of it can also be digital.

Most money today exists online. How else do you pay for Uber Eats or use your credit card? Each time you make an electronic payment, however, your transaction is digitally recorded in one of the databases of a bank or another financial company. You leave a digital footprint on the money that you spend. But let us take a closer look at what exactly a currency is.

Understanding what currency is might seem obvious to people who use it every day. But if you happen to ask them, you may yet be surprised to find out that very few people have a proper understanding of how currency works.

Money solves the problem of bartering and is considered a unit of account. The very fancy term for it would be numeraire—if you would like to impress your friends. Either way, in each country, you use a form of money to exchange it for either a good like a loaf of bread or a service, like getting one's plumbing fixed. Currency can either appear on notes made of paper or coins, and it is just a very convenient way to pay.

Instead of paying two hundred loaves of bread to get your pipes fixed, considering plumbing is quite expensive. I might be exaggerating though.

Now one common form of currency you may know is the U.S Dollar. But there is also the Japanese Yen, the UK's Euro, South Africa's rand, India's Rupie, etc. I could go on and on and on, but we all understand people work with different currencies in different countries.

So, how do you determine a currency's value? Well, taking a look at history, at first many of the coins were made from a variety of different precious metals. But now, the coins and paper notes don't carry as much value themselves per se. So the reason it is valuable is for the following two reasons.

First, your currency could be 'representative money.' What does that mean? You can change your coin or note for a certain commodity. For example, one could exchange 35 dollars for an ounce of gold during World War II. Therefore, the dollar's worth was legally tied to gold.

But the gold supply had many concerns, and President Nixon had decided to cancel the agreement and leave the gold standard behind. This turned the dollar into fiat money, which means it holds its value simply because everyone agrees that it does. It is a weird thought. Much like Peter Pan always believes he can fly, people accept the dollar's value and so does the government and all other countries. Most of the value comes from the trust in the government. Naturally, they want a way to levy as well as collect taxes.

Looking at The Exchange Rate

But an American dollar is not the same value as a Pound. Nor is an Indian Rupee the same value as a Korean Won. How exactly do people work out the exchange rate? I always thought there was some heavy math or logic that runs behind the scenes, and although there are some complexities, the idea behind the exchange rates is quite simple.

There are again two options when it comes to the exchange rate:

- Firstly, a government can link the value of its currency to one of the biggest world currencies. It is meant to help with the stability of their coin and is quite effective in the local exchange rate. It is certainly helpful if a country's financial market is not so complicated, and easy to work with.
- Secondly, a government could choose to let its currency float. This means that it is ultimately up to the market to decide upon its value, now you understand my previous point on people choosing the value of the dollar? Because, it may be obvious now, but a dollar is a floating currency. The bigger the demand in the currency is, the stronger the currency will become. It makes it more expensive for the weaker currencies.

So, then what about inflation? You have likely heard of it. Inflation is a person's worst nightmare at the end of the year. Inflation strikes hard every year. Inflation is known as the measurement of how much prices of goods and services rise each year.

Considering most countries use fiat currencies in this day and age, and they are not linked to any form of a physical asset, they are then prone to inflation. The government has the freedom to print as much money as they want to address any money problems they could be having.

But if they print too much, it causes hyperinflation (when the prices increase like a balloon in the economy). Although it is generally rare, hyperinflation has occurred a couple of times in a couple of countries, such as Germany, Argentina, and Russia.

To avoid hyperinflation, governments sometimes make work of taking money out of the equation if the currency starts to rapidly remove value. So even if you think that printing more money will help the poor economies, in reality, you would bring more harm and good. Now is a good time to understand that the market and the currencies are a little more connected than what most people initially have believed.

Understanding Ledgers

Ledgers are a record-keeping system for financial reasons. Without keeping a good record, how on earth are people supposed to tell whether or not they have made a profit or a loss? How would they know whether or not a debt has been paid or when they have been paying off a debt?

Ledgers these days work on a double booking system. What does that mean? It means that there are two sides to a record. The left side is the debit and the right side is the credit. Each transaction is normally called a journal entry.

And because all entries are placed on debit and credit sides, they all should balance (be the same) when you add the sides.

Every accountant and business has this equation: Assets = Capital - liabilities. Assets are items of value in the business, liabilities are debts, and capital determines the total worth that is put in the business.

The reason why it is so important to understand the ledger is that blockchain, the foundational element of cryptocurrency, works like a ledger, which both transfers all the money from one point to the other but also happens to keep a record of it.

So now you have a great understanding of money. You know how currency works, and why there is a difference in the values which you see. You also now understand that to run an economy, business, or even a household, you will need a record-keeping system to keep things going.

The Distrust in Banks

To also understand cryptocurrency a little better, it is also important to get a brief understanding of the major distrust of banks, and why this sparked the start of Bitcoin and the popularity of many cryptocurrencies.

For example, nearly half of all Americans do not trust banks. People have, slowly but surely, been taking out the money in their savings and using it to invest, save in cash, or find other means to grow their income for their future.

But the high-interest rates from loans and savings accounts that simply do not beat inflation are not cutting it for people. Furthermore, banks unfortunately also have a very negative impact on history, which some people make sure never to forget today.

From the 1980s to the 1990s, banks specifically had a huge crisis and failures, causing over 1,600 banks insured by the FDIC (Federal Deposit Insurance Corporation) to close, and leaving a lot of people in the wake and without their money. The cost of this overall crisis was over $160.1 billion.

Then in the year 2007 to 2008 (which is freakishly not long ago), it had another financial crisis which had been considered as one of the worst ever since the Great Depression's cause of bank failures.

With such a string of bank failures, it leaves people to wonder when the next bank failure could occur and how badly people could be affected by it. Economic depression and crisis are the stuff of nightmares, and if there is a way out, people would surely want to find it.

Now it is time to dive in and introduce you to the primary topic of this whole book, cryptocurrency, how it works, benefits and cons, as well as how to trade. Hang on tight, because there is a whole lot of information to remember!

Chapter 2: What Is Crypto?

What is crypto? What have you heard about it? You have likely heard of Bitcoin. Even I could recall the buzzing rumors arising about Bitcoin and what it could do in the future, and now looking at how far Bitcoin has come, there is no doubt that it has a whole lot of potential.

Bitcoin is the very first cryptocurrency to have been designed by Satoshi Nakamoto. But before we carry on any further in Bitcoin, you need to understand a little about what Bitcoin is.

What is Crypto?

Cryptocurrency is, in the simplest definition, a form of digital money. You will never find a physical coin for Bitcoin. The only reason why people picture it as a coin is that it was given a digital design, and so have many other different cryptocurrencies.

Cryptocurrency runs on a decentralized network called a blockchain. What does it mean to be decentralized? Well, normally in a business, you have a boss who is in charge of how everything runs. This is called a centralized business. But when something is decentralized, then you do not have a singular person or small group of people in control of the software or this case, crypto.

It means also, there is no specific person or group of people who can control cryptocurrency, and by theory, is even immune from the government (I say theoretically because, despite the potential, cryptocurrency still has a fair share of flaws).

Cryptocurrency payments and interactions are all online. You can make a payment on crypto without needing to use a bank or other company such as PayPal (commonly referred to as third-party intermediaries). It means you can directly send money across the globe.

The Foundations of Crypto

So why has crypto become so popular? Yes, it runs online, and you can access it anywhere. But the majority of the time you also have access to online banking and credit cards when making digital payments. So what makes crypto so special?

Benefits of Crypto

- Whenever you make a transaction internationally or to a different bank, you are smacked with a transaction fee. But here comes crypto with a low fee or sometimes no cost at all! Furthermore, you are not bugging anyone out of bed when making the transactions. You can make them anytime, at any place and there are no limits to how many purchases you want to make or withdrawals you'd like to take on.
- Transactions with cryptocurrencies are also a lot faster than a traditional wire transfer. Wire transfers can take about 12 hours (half a day), to move it from point A to point B. But when you bring crypto, it can take a few minutes to even a few seconds (do take note this does depend on the cryptocurrency you are using, as both Bitcoin and Ethereum have at times been a little slow).
- Cryptocurrency is also quite private. What do I mean by this? Well, for anyone who values having complete control over their money as well as wanting to keep their identity hidden online, then cryptocurrency is a great advantage.
- High risks call for bigger rewards, cryptocurrency is known to be a risky investment, and they are known to have quick spikes as well as sudden drops in their value. It

all greatly depends on supply and demand. Either way, people who play their cards well are capable of earning a good amount of money from investing in crypto.

- The blockchain technology on which crypto runs is known to be secure. Online transactions are known for being targets of hackers, and sometimes having interference while a transaction is made. However, when a transaction is made on crypto, it is known to be tamper-proof and will be explained later when we delve deeper into the blockchain.

- But despite their security, blockchain is also quite transparent. Most businesses, banks, and companies are not nearly as transparent as they should be. But with the blockchain, anyone can see the transactions that are taking place. You can see it, I can see it, someone from halfway around the world can see it. They only need internet transactions, and it calls for a more honest atmosphere. Honesty builds trust and in turn allows people to more easily work with the company, business, or even website.

Cons of Crypto

But despite all of these advantages of crypto, there is always a flipside. Every design will always have a flaw. I bet that whenever you make a drawing or come up with an idea, it is never perfect. There will always be a downside. Not that it should stop you, but it allows you to be cautious and make wiser choices. It is very important to understand the other side of crypto, and most people investing in crypto simply want to ignore it, or never highlight it while encouraging you to invest. But without knowing the cons, how on earth can you make sure to avoid most of the flaws?

- Working and investing in cryptocurrency takes time and energy. It is not exactly a passive form of income, especially not in the beginning. Especially when you want to learn about this digital technology and don't have much prior knowledge. The less you know about something, the riskier it is to invest.
- Cryptocurrencies' volatility is both a gift and a curse. What does volatility mean? It means how easy or how difficult an item is to predict, as well as how quickly it can change. The more volatile an item is, the quicker it can change without warning. And cryptocurrency runs on a lot of speculation and many empty predictions.
- Crypto has not had the time to prove itself as a trustworthy investment. Cryptocurrency is

merely a teenager, with Bitcoin being launched in 2008. However, stock markets have existed for centuries, considering that the London Stock Exchange had been founded in the year 1801. So, due to crypto's incredibly short-track record, no one can tell where it will head into the future.

- People who are new to crypto are more vulnerable to risks. Although other investments do also have equal risks, people investing in crypto need to stay wide awake, alert, and push up their security. As hackers love to try and steal your passwords through various tricks and schemes. Be very careful about the websites you visit and the information you give. Never share your private key with anyone.

- Cryptocurrency does have issues with scalability. What does this mean? Well, cryptocurrency has only recently become popular, but most payments and money are still going through the regular banks/financial companies, Visa and Mastercard. Cryptocurrency does not have the structure to take on a larger amount of people. It means the more people who climb onto specific crypto, the slower the transaction rate will go. Does it sound a lot like modern-day traffic in cities? Yep, that pretty much sums up how blockchain transactions work when too many people want to use crypto. And because of how volatile crypto is, you want to have speed in both your purchases and when you sell your tokens (Tokens are the coins of cryptocurrencies).

Trading in Crypto - Top Tips

So what should you do if you want to trade with cryptocurrency? Is there a secret trading step-by-step manual that everyone should follow to be successful? I wish there was, I do, but cryptocurrency is so incredibly young that even the experts are still trying to figure out how it works.

You have experts claiming that crypto is going to succeed and take over.

But you also have experts saying the cryptocurrency is going to fail.

So which is it?

Well, no one knows for sure. For now, all we can do is watch and wait, if not, perhaps take a little part in trading and investing in crypto to see what all the hype is about as well as earn us a little money. So here are the top tips traders have given when working with crypto:

- Have a goal in mind when you trade. Having a purpose allows you to make a plan and push yourself towards it. Understand that working with crypto, there will always be someone who is going to win and someone who is going to lose.
- Set up a plan beforehand on how much you are willing to lose before pulling out of the market,

and also how much you are going to win before pulling out. And remember to stick to it. Most of the time people feel lucky, but end up with a hefty loss (which would have been a profit if they pulled out earlier). Others seem to push, constantly growing their loss in hopes to make up some of the money. Sometimes it is better to pack up, call it a day and return in the morning refreshed and far less emotionally motivated.

- Be very careful of FOMO (fear of missing out). This is when a market rushes to buy into a cryptocurrency with no good reason. Be very careful of the communities and it is always better to question a crowd than to follow along blindly.

- Diversification is a good goal. What does that mean? Well, buying more than just one coin. Because of cryptocurrencies' unpredictable nature, it is best to diversify and buy different coins. That way you are spreading the risks. Most investors and traders work with a broad portfolio (the collection of their investments and earnings) that allows them to be successful as well as take smaller losses if something were to fail.

- When starting to trade, you have to learn how to read charts. Reading charts allows you to pick up trends, implement strategies and just get a great idea of which direction a specific cryptocurrency is heading. Charts may seem puzzling, but it is not that hard to learn. It gives you a mental picture of the price value, and there is a reason why you learned about charts in math or are still learning.

- Take on trading and investment strategies that have been tried and true. You do not have to stumble in the dark learning how to earn money while trading. People have shared some of the most popular as well as sensible trading strategies. Don't be scared to use them! They are there for a reason, and it is best to use strategies as a beginner that experts are still using, allowing you to build up the necessary experience. Could you change some strategies? Sure! AFTER you have picked up on experience. Very much like an artist learning the rules of drawing, it is only fair to break them after they have had the necessary practice to become good in art.

- When starting with cryptocurrency investments, it is best to start with long-term investment strategies. It takes a lot more practice and experience to partake in day trading, so why not take your time investing long-term and learning about the daily markets at the same time?

Working with cryptocurrency is a little different to other forms of investments. Because you are working with a digital asset, and also a very new one at that. It means there will always be a level of uncertainty as we move into the future. No one can guarantee that crypto is going to last, but neither can people say that crypto is doomed to fail. When looking at the risks and the benefits, you will come to realize that it can go both ways. It is entirely up to the future decisions that the market makes in order to determine that.

There you have it, both the good and the dark side of crypto. But how exactly does crypto run? You are now familiar with how money works, and that crypto is digital money. Now let us take a look at the digital ledger which runs the foundation of crypto, and is the most complicated concept of crypto: blockchain.

Chapter 3: What Is Blockchain?

You understand a ledger. It is a record of transactions. Do you keep a good track of your purchases? Some people are better at it than others, but blockchain does the recording for you.

Now, I need you to concentrate when reading this chapter. The good news is unless you are planning on becoming a crypto miner, it is only necessary that you understand the basics of blockchain. Either way, there is still a good chunk of information you need to know to fully understand how blockchain works.

Blockchain Simplified

First, let us visit the entire goal of what blockchain is built on. This factor plays a role as to why blockchain works so incredibly well, and why people would love to see blockchain running many other systems other than crypto. This factor would be trusted.

The best way to explain blockchain is to give you a mental picture. Imagine there is this big red house. Well, how do you keep track of its value? Well, you keep a ledger of course! Imagine that this book records the times the house has been bought, the times the house has been sold, and any repairs made to the house. An example of a repair would be when the chimney was fixed, thus adding to the value of the house.

The problem is, if you have a book, what is one problem with having such a record? Well, it is very easy to change the record and to lie. You could simply mention that the house has been repainted when in reality that has never happened. Or, you want to remove the record that rats had to be exterminated. It is very easy to change it, especially if the book is in your hands.

How can you solve the problem from someone messing with the book? Well, this is where you give the book to a third party, such as a real estate agent or a bank that keeps a record of what exactly is happening to the house. But here is another problem: people can still bribe bankers to change the record. Now, this just won't do.

And here is where blockchain comes in. It is a digital ledger, which works as follows:

You have a transaction that happens. All this information is placed in a 'block' of information. Once this block of information has been created, it creates a special key. But here is where you need to focus. If you change the information in this block of information, the design of the special key changes. The keys do not look at all the same.

Now a second transaction is made. You have a second block of information. But, you also have block 1s special key placed in block 2, before block 2's special key is designed. So if any information of block 2's information is changed, the design of block 2's key will change. Also, if block 1's key's design were to change (because block 1's information has been changed), what do you think will happen to block 2's key? It will also change.

The same happens when a third transaction is made. The keys of blocks 1 and 2 are placed in the third block alongside the information, and thus blockchain's 3rd key is made.

So now you have a string of information linked together, and here is where it gets a little tricky again. But there is not just one string, but hundreds of copies of the same string of information stored in different computers. And every ten minutes or so, the computers 'sync' or check up on each other to make sure all the information is correct. So if one or two strings are different in comparison to the majority of copies of the blockchain information, then the two different strings will automatically be updated to the majority's information.

So although blockchain is not hacker-proof, it is incredibly easy to see when something has been tampered with. It works like a shining beacon in the middle of the night that something is just off. This is why blockchain is called 'tamper-proof.'

So what exactly are these keys? Well, they will be explained in chapter 9 with Crypto mining. These keys are called hashes, and how they work is incredibly smart.

Blockchain Analogy

I am now going to paint another two mental pictures for you to make 100% sure you truly understand how blockchain works.

Glass Box Analogy

Fabricio Santos explained blockchain with the analogy of a glass box. Imagine you are standing in a bank vault filled with rows and rows of unlabeled boxes. But instead of metal, each box is made up of glass. You can see exactly what the contents are inside.

However, no one can just simply open and access it. An individual owner needs a key specifically made for that box. But just because someone has the key does not mean the box belongs to the keyholder. But the person who owns the key can access the contents inside of the box.

Blockchain works a lot like this, like a bunch of linked glass boxes, everyone can see what is going on inside, as well as verify the information. But they are unable to change it.

Google Docs

Another analogy that I am particularly fond of is the Google Docs analogy. If you have worked with Google Docs before, this will be easy to understand.

Imagine you are working on a document as a group. But if you were to work on Microsoft Word, there will be a lot of back and forth going on. One singular person works on that document and sends it to another. This person types in the edits and comments and sends them back. Either way, a lot of waiting and a lot of time is wasted when taking this on.

But if you work on Google Docs, you will be able to access and collaborate with anyone who has access to the document in real-time. Every person can view it, and make various comments or suggest changes, and even the history of the documents is available to be viewed.

This is exactly how blockchain also works, but instead of a shared document, it is a shared ledger. People can verify the information and comment about it, but direct changes cannot be made to the information which has already been placed in and verified.

Blockchain Reality

Every single cryptocurrency runs on blockchain. But blockchain is truly an infant, and there is a whole lot more to be learned about blockchain. There is a lot of speculation about where the cryptocurrency may go, but there seems a level of certainty that blockchain is here to stay due to its technology. Why? because of what blockchain can do for us and its economy.

The possibilities that run on the blockchain are truly endless, and here are some of the top possibilities as well as innovations that have indeed come with blockchain technology:

- NFTs - Non-Fungible Tokens will be discussed in Chapter 10, although NFTs did arise in 2014, they have only truly taken the stage in the last few years. With the potential it has for passive income, we are going to be seeing and hearing more about NFTs in the future.
- Faster transactions - Without the compromise of security. If blockchain were to be adopted as more financial means of making transactions, then we will see an average spike in transaction speeds as well as a higher level of transparency within businesses. Transparency is all too necessary in a distrusting society. And it is not as if people don't trust banks and companies for no reason either. Take a look at history and you

can fully understand why people have such a negative viewpoint in the centralized companies that pretty much run our economy.

- Digital identity - We all use our passwords and other methods of authentication to safely verify our identity online. But blockchain could help establish a safer, more secure digital identity online.
- Health Records - Blockchain does not just have to be a digital ledger of money, but digital identities, as well as the health of a person, could be recorded in blockchain technology. So if healthcare providers were to make use of blockchain, it would improve the speeds where doctors and nurses can find the necessary information about a person's medical history to come up with a quicker diagnosis of what is wrong with a person. When it comes to someone's health, everyone knows that timing is truly everything.

There you have it! A sneak peek at blockchain and the future that it holds. However, people adopting new technology especially on a global scale is always known to be quite slow. So don't be expecting blockchain to take over the world in one or two years. It might even take a good decade or two before blockchain has a firm hold in technology. Either way, hopefully by now, you have a greater understanding of how blockchain works, and we can move on to the original cryptocurrency that shook the world and brought a whole new level of technology to the table.

Chapter 4: What Is Bitcoin?

Bitcoin is a cryptocurrency, and it is the very first of its kind. That is why any cryptocurrency that is not Bitcoin is called an altcoin. It was launched in January 2009 by a pseudonym of Satoshi Nakamoto. Why do I say pseudonym?

Well, no one knows who Satoshi Nakamoto is, and whether or not it is one person or a group of people. Apart from different speculations, people are yet to discover the face behind one of the biggest inventions in the early 2000s.

Bitcoin is a type of cryptocurrency because it makes use of cryptography to make sure it is secure, and there is no physical coin you can touch or see from Bitcoin. It is 100% digital.

Transactions on Bitcoin are all verified through computer power processes called mining, and it is also important to know that it is not backed by any banks or governments. Therefore it is not a legal tender, but Bitcoin's popularity has taken the world by storm. Shortly after Bitcoin was launched, thousands of others flocked in to make cryptocurrencies of their own.

And how on earth could they copy Bitcoin's design? Well, considering that blockchain and Bitcoin are open-source. People have access to the design and software completely for free.

Bitcoin is also given the abbreviation of BTC on the different trading platforms.

Origin of Bitcoin

Let us take a look at the timeline of Bitcoin, and how far it has come since its origin in 2009.

- In the year 2008, Bitcoin.org had been registered, and there is no information on the identity of the person who had registered the domain.
- In October 2008, Satoshi Nakamoto made the public announcement that they have made and are working on a form of electronic cash system. They also stated that it was peer-to-peer, and people did not have to make use of a trusted third party.
- January 3rd, 2009, the very first Bitcoin block had been mined. This blockchain was called the 'genesis block' as it was the very first block of the blockchain.
- January 8th-9th 2009, the very first original version of Bitcoin software had been publicly announced on the mailing list of Cryptography. And 1 blockchain had been mined which meant that Bitcoin mining had started as well.

Design of Bitcoin

Bitcoin is run on a variety of different computers. These computers are normally called nodes, or sometimes miners. They are the ones that run Bitcoin's code and they also store the blockchain on their computers, thus why I said there are many copies of blockchain on a variety of different computers scattered all across the globe.

However, everyone can see the transactions that are happening in real-time, and if you are scared of someone perhaps taking control of Bitcoin, well here is why it would be so difficult. For someone to change blockchain on Bitcoin, they would need to have control of 51% of all the computers holding onto Bitcoin.

And there are about 14,000 computers, more or less, running Bitcoin. So the likelihood of someone pulling off such an attack is highly unlikely, and here is the deal to sweeten the pot. Even if someone could pull off a hack to control over 7,000 computers, the miners would simply split off and create a new blockchain, making the attacker's efforts a complete waste.

Bitcoin tokens, the coins of Bitcoin, are held by making use of both public and private 'keys.' They are just a long string of numbers and letters and are linked to a very specific encryption algorithm. The public key of Bitcoin works a whole lot like a bank account number and works as the address for people to send their payments to. So if you were to send Bitcoin to someone, you would make use of their public key.

The private key works a lot like a bank pin, and you must not share the private key of your cryptocurrency with anyone. They are the ones that allow you to make payments with your Bitcoin. If someone else were to get their hands on it, or if you were to lose it, then that Bitcoin you own is lost forever.

Peer-to-Peer Technology

Peer-to-peer, otherwise known as P2P, is known as the instant payments that are made. You make a payment directly to someone else, without a bank, or company. You are in charge of sending the money directly where it needs to go.

When you make a transaction, it is, however, verified by miners in the Bitcoin Network. They are rewarded for their hard work with Bitcoins or money of their own.

Pros and Cons

The design of Bitcoin shocked the world, but it was not a perfect system, and although Bitcoin's benefits ride on the benefits of cryptocurrency that had been mentioned, there are a few matters and cons that should be addressed about Bitcoin:

- Bitcoin is a risky investment because it is volatile and there is no regulation. Without regulation and rules, it can make something pretty risky as well as allow the wrong types of people to use it.
- Security risks: Most people use Bitcoin on exchange or broker apps ,online platforms that are indeed centralized), but that does mean they are frequently targets of hackers, scammers, and more. Even if they are not hacked, if the exchange is hacked, they still risk the chance of losing everything.
- Market risk: The values of Bitcoin will always fluctuate. This means that it jumps in value, then drops. Think of a balloon that is not tied. You blow air and it quickly swells up, but if you release the balloon, it quickly loses its size. Consider Bitcoin's value working a little like this. This is why it is hard to know for certain what will happen with Bitcoin.
- Bitcoin's community is also not so united, and there are many times in which people have disagreed and split within the community. And even in some instances, a large group of users, as well as miners, have changed some of the Bitcoin protocols running in the Bitcoin protocol.

Understanding Bitcoin's Value

So if it keeps jumping in prices, the communities argue, and it is not backed by the government, why is Bitcoin still so incredibly valuable? Well, there is no denying the price of Bitcoin has risen to a huge amount in just a decade. Its value was less than 1 dollar in the year 2011, and in November 2021, it became more than $68,000 in value.

Well, it all falls under supply and demand. Bitcoin is relatively scarce, there is a higher demand in the market and the cost of production is quite high. Therefore, Bitcoin does have a high valuation. Its market cap, the total of all Bitcoin's combined, is valued to be over $1.11 trillion in November 2021. This is also why, despite all the problems Bitcoin has, it has still been going strong.

Where Bitcoin Is Headed

So which way is Bitcoin headed? Is it going to survive, or is the competition going to take over in the future? Is Bitcoin just one big scam?

Even though Bitcoin cannot be physically touched or handled, it is real. Considering it has been around for over a decade, there is no denying Bitcoin's existence, and the system has been proving to be robust as it can handle big ups and downs. Bitcoin is also completely transparent. So although there are a great many issues with fraudsters and con artists trying to scam people out of their crypto, there is nothing wrong with Cryptocurrency itself.

There is also a total amount of 21 million Bitcoins, and it is said that it will be fully mined in the year 2140.

But recently, there are many warnings that Bitcoin might not last that long, and it is not necessarily for the reasons you may think.

Bitcoin runs on computer processing power, although this will be better explained in the chapters in regards to mining, computer power takes a lot of energy and electricity. Which in turn, contributes to the environmental damage. And the world is becoming far more aware that changes need to be made in how cities are run to have positive changes to the climate. Therefore, the popularity of Bitcoin is slowly but surely reducing.

A few years ago, there used to be just a few cryptocurrencies competing with Bitcoin, but now there are hundreds that are more useful than Bitcoin and are known to be environmentally friendly in the way that it runs.

How Bitcoin uses blockchain technology is not as efficient as many other cryptocurrencies have managed to use it. The carbon footprint Bitcoin leaves are larger than the whole country of New Zealand.

Although it is not likely for cryptocurrency to die out, we are likely to see a change in popularity and see a slow but steady decline in Bitcoin's value.

As much as this is a very negative viewpoint, Bitcoin has survived a few rough hurdles. Many expected to see Bitcoin crash once China closed its doors towards this cryptocurrency. However, Bitcoin not only survived but also thrived despite losing a huge chunk of its users.

Although Bitcoin does not have the power to take down the dollar or centralized banks, the way it runs is changing how we make payments. And Bitcoin's network is still ever-changing. It means that Bitcoin does have the capability to change for the better, and keep its number 1 title.

In reality, it will take the next decade to understand Bitcoin's future. Which makes predicting Bitcoin incredibly complicated. It is such a mix of both incredibly beneficial as well as critical viewpoints, that no one can tell you for certain which way Bitcoin may go. However, there are three major possibilities:

1. Bitcoin's network can efficiently change and adapt to the environmental needs, have reduced volatility and greater adoption, become the world's digital gold, and have other cryptocurrencies and stable coins also take charge of digital payments while having greater regulations. The government and other governing bodies have better control of how

cryptocurrency is run to reduce volatility as well as cybercrime.

2. Bitcoin's popularity will continue declining. More and more people will start adopting other, safer, and better cryptocurrencies. Bitcoin will be the originator and take its place in history as the originator, but give up its value.

3. Bitcoin and the other cryptocurrencies will fail, leading to devastating consequences on the economy and rocking the market. If crypto as a whole were to fail, it would leave a dark impact on the world due to the value it holds to this day.

As you can see, the possibilities are complete opposites. All that you can do is wait, and see and decide for yourself where you think Bitcoin is headed alongside all the other cryptocurrencies. There is not much else a person can do, but steer clear of crypto or take part, and see what role it will start playing in the future. Do remember, cash and money have been around for over a thousand years, whereas Bitcoin and cryptocurrency this past decade. So it is fair to give it a bit more time to have a proper understanding of what direction it will head towards.

But for now, we can take a look and see all the other cryptocurrencies that have started to shine in the world of crypto, as well as hold the potential of taking over Bitcoin's throne.

Chapter 5: What Are Altcoins?

Now as mentioned in the previous chapter, altcoins are cryptocurrencies designed after Bitcoin. There are many of them out there, as basically, anyone with the right skills and motivation can design a cryptocurrency as the information is freely available.

There are thousands of cryptocurrencies out there. More are being made each year and the term altcoins is a reference to any type or form of cryptocurrency other than Bitcoin.

In January 2022, there had been a record of 16,500 cryptocurrencies, and Bitcoin makes nearly half of the total market cap of all cryptocurrencies. Ethereum makes up about a quarter. It means that all other cryptocurrencies share about 40% of the total value of cryptocurrency.

Altcoins Investing Explained

Other cryptocurrencies have taken to the field of popularity, such as Ethereum, XRP, Tether, Cardano, Polkadot, and Stellar.

If you are wondering whether or not you should invest in altcoins, there are a few matters you do need to take into consideration. Cryptocurrency is a risky investment. So any money you put in, you should be able to afford to lose it. If you walk into cryptocurrency with that rule and attitude in mind, then you are quite safe for investing in crypto.

Cryptocurrency, especially, is not a get-rich-quick scheme as many people paint it out to be. To be successful in altcoins, you need to take the time and effort to learn as much about it as you can. Learning trading strategies, learning about the coin itself, who runs it, and what plans it has in the future is a very important matter to adopt.

Many experts have said that cryptocurrency is here to stay, but that does not mean all 16,000 cryptocurrencies are going to survive the future hurdles. The majority of cryptocurrencies fail, which is why you need to be careful in your choices of investing. Especially if you are new to trading, it is best to err on the side of caution.

Many experts also recommend keeping crypto to about 5% of your entire portfolio, due to the risk that it holds. Sure high risks hold for high rewards, but you have to play the game with the mindset that you could lose, and not necessarily by your fault either, but simply a jolt in social media can turn the tables upside down for you.

Why is Cryptocurrency So Volatile?

This may lead you to ask why is cryptocurrency so risky, but so popular?

The biggest reason why the cryptocurrency is so incredibly volatile is because of how new it still is. Although it has caught the eye of many investors, the risk is keeping many people away.

New ideas take time to take as well as be accepted. Although crypto has gained a lot of power and popularity worldwide, they are still not accepted as a traditional asset such as gold or equity. The longer cryptocurrency lasts and matures, the more it will be accepted over time.

There is also an incredible lack of rules and regulations considering crypto's new nature. And people are still just trying to figure out how exactly crypto works and what part it can play in society. Don't get me wrong, there are a lot of ideas, but ideas don't work unless an action plan is in place.

Here are the other common factors leading to crypto's volatile nature:

- There is no controlling agency for crypto like fiat, bonds, or equities are. It means that the value of cryptocurrency purely relies on what the market believes it to be. And if you know anything about the market, people, and social media, they change their minds very quickly.

- Sentimental factor - Many investors are buying and selling cryptocurrency based on sentiment. For me, a classic example would be the Dogecoin cryptocurrency. This crypto was built for a joke and based on a meme. It was never meant to take off so well, but due to sentiment and Elon Musk's tweets, Dogecoin is still running strong, despite not having as many benefits as many other cryptocurrencies do.
- There is a limited supply of certain cryptocurrencies, but a small number of people own the limited supply. Considering cryptocurrency runs on the laws of supply and demand, if there were only a few people who owned the majority of the cryptocurrency, then they have a great amount of control over the value of the crypto. This is a common factor with Bitcoin.
- Social media's power - Fake or real news can trigger the direction in which a cryptocurrency goes. It is exactly why social media is such a ripe field of scammers and con artists, where they love to post lies about cryptocurrency, hoping to manipulate the market in their favor. And sometimes it works, causing many investors to make large losses. Market manipulation in crypto is fairly easy because of its unregulated nature.

Etherium

Etherium takes second place in the leading cryptocurrencies, and that is why it is getting its special place in this chapter. Ethereum has a lot of potentials, and as mentioned before, takes up a quarter of the total value of cryptocurrency.

Ethereum is also a decentralized blockchain. It works the same as Bitcoin with the peer-to-peer network. But it also has other advantages. You can do more than just transactions on Ethereum. You can also insert and work with smart contracts.

What are smart contracts? They are codes in the Ethereum platform that allow people to make transactions with each other without needing a central authority. Smart contracts can release payments to a person once a certain digital requirement is met.

Ethereum is a flexible platform, and it has its token called Ether. Developers and investors take great interest in Ether because of all the advantages it brings to the table.

Ethereum is also the main home of NFTs that will be explained in Chapter 10.

You can also build your cryptocurrencies using Ethereum, and some of the most popular cryptocurrencies have come originally from the

Ethereum platform to give you an idea of how well the platform works.

Any transactions or payments that need to be made on Ethereum are paid through its token called Ether. Ether makes sure to prevent any unnecessary transactions from taking place on the Ethereum platform, and it gives incentive to people who want to participate in mining.

Ethereum is very often compared to Bitcoin, as they do share a variety of similarities. But they also share a wide variety of differences. Ethereum is known to be one of the world's best programmable blockchains, which means you can do so much more on the platform, with an unlimited amount of Ethers.

Ethereum's protocol on how blockchain runs is also slowly changing its protocol to use a whole lot less computer energy, thus having a far more environmentally friendly impact. Ethereum was also a very guilty cryptocurrency in regards to how much power it was using to run.

Popular Altcoins

Other than Ethereum, there are quite a few other altcoins that you can consider investing in. I will, however, only be giving a very brief summary of how they work. If you truly want to invest in a specific coin,

I highly advise you to go dig deeper on the internet, but steer clear of social media. It is a great platform to pick up on trends, but the worst platform in picking up verified information and advice.

- Lucky Block is a crypto platform that works on impacting the lottery industry. It also has a built-in burn rate—where they store crypto tokens in places it can never be used, essentially getting rid of a token—which in summary means that if the supply of these tokens decreases, the value of the tokens will keep growing naturally.
- Aave - This is a cryptocurrency that helps you to lend as well as borrow cryptocurrencies without too much difficulty. This allows you to implement some great trading strategies to earn a good amount of money.
- Stellar - This network that has very fast payments, extremely low fees, and a great system is known to improve the traditional banking system.
- Cardano - This is crypto built on research. It is the cryptocurrency with some of the best potentials, as it has the same elements as Ethereum, and has been peer-reviewed by a variety of different experts to iron out all the flaws that haunt cryptocurrencies. However, it's developing very slowly and still very much behind Ethereum's technology.
- Ripple - Ripple also offers cheap and fast transfers of money in comparison to banks and can be considered as a bridge to users

worldwide. Ripple's payments are almost instant, and it is likely to pick up in its popularity over the years to come.

Caution Story of New Altcoins

If you want to take your chance with altcoins, hoping to strike it lucky as many did when they invested in Bitcoin, you need to understand a couple of things, and practice caution. Investing in altcoins can work an awful lot like a gamble, especially if you do not put in enough time and research into understanding how cryptocurrency works.

Understanding ICO

Most cryptocurrencies start by raising money through Initial Coin Offerings. This is where investors can see all the different cryptocurrency projects, even those that have not yet been launched, and invest in hopes to strike it lucky.

But scams are riddling the ICO marketplace, where they make incredible promises, only to be leaving you in the dust after enough investments have been made.

New Altcoins Are in the Biggest Danger

The newer the altcoin, the greater danger there is to fail. This is because it still needs to pick up on its popularity, and hasn't managed to prove itself yet. New altcoins also fall victim to pump and dump schemes. This is where people use social media to make others believe a certain altcoin is going to become incredibly popular. Investors flock in, shooting the value of the crypto, and the scammers leave, allowing the altcoin to crash in value, the scammers have the extra money in their pockets, and investors leave bitter, never looking twice at that altcoin again

When investing in altcoins, you need to look up both the benefits and the cons. Find out the risks and the rewards. Dig and discover the people behind a specific cryptocurrency, and find out what experience they have when it comes to crypto.

The more transparent a cryptocurrency is, the better it is for you. If you cannot even find the bare minimum of information, then you should steer far away. Never invest in a crypto that promises guaranteed returns. Why? Because realistically, no one can guarantee that no matter what investment they are making.

We will be delving a little later on how to stay safe in cryptocurrency and avoid the most common scams, but now you have a greater understanding of altcoins, how they work, and what to be aware of. While you are still inexperienced, it is best to stick to investing in some of the top altcoins, staying safe with what is tried and true. The younger and newer an altcoin is, the greater the risk. And if you do not have the experience, then it is incredibly easy to miss the warning signs that come with trading dangerous crypto.

So be gracious with yourself, and give yourself the necessary time and practice to become more experienced with investing in crypto. Much like anything else, trading and investing is more than a hobby, it is a skill, and the more you practice and are open to learning, the better off you will be in the future.

But now, it is time to take a look at a cryptocurrency that has been designed to cut out the biggest disadvantage that crypto has: its volatility.

Chapter 6: What Are Stablecoins?

Stablecoins do belong in a different category in cryptocurrency. Why? Because they are designed differently. Stablecoins are designed to be less risky and have far more stability than other forms of cryptocurrency. And it seems like they have become incredibly popular for it.

What Are Stablecoins?

What exactly are stable coins and why have they become so popular? Well, stablecoins try to be the best of both worlds. They have access to the security and privacy offered by a cryptocurrency, but at the same time stay free of volatility. How do they manage this? Well, they tie their value to another asset like gold, dollars, or other options.

Although Bitcoin still has the number one ranking, it is known for its high volatility and price jumps. I have mentioned this to you quite a few times, and it must be drilled in. All these price swings can give a perfectly healthy person a headache and is one of the biggest reasons why people do not want to work with crypto. And who can blame them? They live with the chance of going to bed rich and waking up with all their money gone.

It also makes cryptocurrency unsuitable for the general public. The majority of people do not want to work with something whose value can change within minutes of an event. The ideal scenario is to have cryptocurrency have low inflation and keep the same level of purchasing power that can allow people to comfortably spend their tokens instead of just saving or using them for trading all the time, and this is what stablecoins intend to provide.

Different Types of Stablecoins

People still use fiat currencies because they are backed by the government. It means that the price of the money will remain stable, but it is still controlled by the central banks. Stablecoins try to act as the bridge between cryptocurrencies and fiat currencies, and the companies that run the stablecoins are regularly audited. This means third parties come and check their records to make sure they are being 100% honest and transparent to their users.

Most stablecoins are backed by fiat currency like the US dollar. It means that these stablecoins have the same stability as fiat currency. Other stablecoins are backed by gold or silver, or even commodities such as oil, but the most popular would remain the fiat currencies.

Why does it need to be audited? For stablecoins to work, it means that they lean towards being centralized—controlled by a small group of individuals. But because stablecoins are competing with cryptocurrencies, it means they also have to prove their trustworthiness. That is exactly why they have their records checked, and hopefully win over the trust of the people.

Pros of Stablecoins

- The biggest advantage stablecoins do bring to the table is the decreased risk. Naturally not everyone wants to play with fire while investing. Stability is a big plus, no matter what investment you want to make, and thus it is one of the leading advantages stablecoins do happen to have over all the other cryptocurrencies.
- Stablecoins are a safe investment choice because they are backed by fixed assets. It means that you don't have to worry about price swings or fake news on social media to cause a dip in your investment. Rather, you can focus on the fiat currency your stablecoin is tied to,

and see which direction that currency is heading.

- Stablecoins do allow for cheaper international payments. So along with the stability, you can still majorly benefit from the international payments for which cryptocurrencies are renowned and praised. Making payments globally is still incredibly easy to do, and just allows you to enjoy some of the benefits that cryptocurrency holds without so much stress of the risks cryptocurrency brings to the table.

Cons of Stablecoins

- Again, no system is perfect. You need to understand this whenever you walk into anything, including a metal pole, but mostly when walking into investments, passive income ideas, and cryptocurrency. Although stablecoins do have a reduced amount of risk, they will never have the same amount of stability that a fiat currency holds, regardless of whether or not the stablecoins are linked.
- Stablecoins are still centralized. It means that they are not nearly as transparent as their decentralized crypto brothers and sisters. For anyone seeking full freedom from banks and

centralized systems, stablecoins are most
certainly not for them.

- A lack of transparency. Stablecoins such as
Tether have received a lot of backlash, as they do
not remain accountable or as transparent as
they should be. They have even been under
investigation by the US Government and had to
settle a lawsuit. Stablecoins are capable of
hiding more than decentralized crypto, and this
is often the reason why people do not want to
invest in stablecoins or centralized companies.
- Stablecoins might become less important if
cryptocurrency as a whole were to grow, mature,
and become less volatile without the need of
pegging their value onto another asset. The less
demand there is for something, the less likely it
will survive. Although this future cannot be
predicted 100%, there is always that possibility.
It is a great future for crypto but will harm all
stablecoins that have been designed, as it takes
away their primary advantage.

Most Popular Stablecoins

There are many stablecoins out there, and if you are
interested in investing, it might be good to check them
out and see all the different advantages they bring to
the table. Just remember to keep in mind why

stablecoins are so popular as well as keep track of the direction cryptocurrency is headed when investing or making use of the stable coin.

Tether

Tether has been ranked amongst the top ten cryptocurrencies. Which is proof of how much people want to have a stable form of crypto that they can use. It has over a $78 billion market cap and is the largest stablecoin out there. Tether was launched in the year 2012 and is based on the US dollar. One token of Tether is the value of one US dollar.

However, Tether has been slightly controversial and because of this, other stablecoins have risen for your consideration.

USD Coin

Just like Tether, it is connected to the US dollar and has been considered popular enough to have the potential of replacing Bitcoin. It is regulated by the US financial institution and has been backed by a stable fiat currency as well.

Binance USD

This is also one of the top stablecoins around, and is also linked to the US dollar. It is well known as one of the best stable choices on investments and even approved by the New York State Department of Financial Services according to (Sinha, 2021).

Dai

This is a new and growing stablecoin tethered to the US dollar (1:1 ratio) and has many financial features such as borrowing, lending, and trading. It is a very popular choice due to the benefits it provides investors when they are making their transactions.

TrueUSD

Also linked 1:1 to the US dollar, TrueUSD is considered to be one of the most liquid (easily converted into cash) stablecoins around. It has the potential of replacing Bitcoin in the future and offers decreased transaction fees in comparison to others. It works hard on its transparency, reliability, and stability with its token and has the potential of taking over many of the traders, commerce, long-term financial contracts, etc.

Stablecoins holds a lot of potential including the benefits of both having crypto slightly more regulated while reflecting a very transparent environment for its users. If more businesses were held to the same standard that a stablecoin was, we would see a far more honest economic environment.

However, the future of stablecoin is truly uncertain. This is because a lot of people are still not a fan of centralized digital currencies, thus making stablecoins go against the main goal of crypto. If other answers were provided to improve cryptocurrency's stability, then the entire use of stablecoin would vanish in an instant. Or people would just start adopting more and more stablecoin, believing that it is truly better than the risky Bitcoin and other decentralized cryptos. Only time will tell.

But a part of me does believe that decentralized and centralized cryptos will always be hanging around. Just because they are different doesn't mean that only one will survive. People love having a variety of choices, and it certainly is a reflection of all the different shops, brands, and similar items with small differences that are being sold. Being able to find a cryptocurrency suitable to your needs and wishes is ideal, and stablecoins provide a lot of security to those unable to handle the risk of other cryptocurrencies.

Chapter 7: Cybercrime With Crypto

Watch out! There are a lot of thieves online, and the problem is, you can't always see it. I always imagine the online realm to be the same as seeing a wolf putting on a sheep's skin, walking around to find unsuspecting victims.

There is a lot to look out for with online safety, and hackers/fraudsters are one of the biggest threats people working with cryptocurrency had to deal with. Here is one common fact that you should know:

Most scammers and thieves can only steal from you if you open the door for them.

That is why they are so good at lying, designing their emails or websites to look almost identical to the real sites, and more. But if you learn to avoid most of the scams and look out for the signs, then you are far less likely to lose the war against scammers who want your money.

Common Scams Online

- You may find a lot of companies making empty promises over the fact that you can earn a whole lot of money in a very short time-span to be free of your 9-5 job. But I have said this once, and I will say it again, cryptocurrency is not a quick-rich scheme if you want to succeed, and steer clear of anyone who promises you guaranteed results in investing.

- Scammers also try to tell you to make patents in cryptocurrency to recruit other people into the program. If you do what they ask, then you will receive rewards each time you get someone to join in. Here is the problem, this is a classic pyramid scheme, full of fake promises, and they will disappear almost as quickly as they have arrived.
- Scammers have the nasty habit of giving advice that you did not ask for and make the appearance of an investment manager. They will give you all sorts of tips and tricks, but if you try and log in to the investment account they have opened for you, you will not be able to withdraw any of your money until you pay a certain fee.

Be careful of the following claims. There is a saying that goes: if it seems too good to be true, then it isn't. Because no matter how much people wish to earn money and find an easy life, cryptocurrency and investing just don't work this way. Sure, some people are lucky. But it is the same luck in which some people win the lottery.

1. Guarantees in making money - Scammer
2. Free money if you just - Scammer
3. Big payouts and guaranteed returns - Scammer

4. Big claims without explanations on how - Scammer

If you find someone making big promises or claims, you really should ask yourself one simple question: how on earth do they get money from it?

If you do not see a way that they can profit with the promises they are making to you, then you can be pretty sure it is a scam. Very few people rarely offer information, advice, or money without another motive at hand. A classic example is free seminars people offer online teaching people how to earn money. Once you watch a seminar, you are bombarded with maybe one or two pieces of good advice, advertisements for their company or brand, and how making payments will allow you to start earning money.

Other Common Scammer Tactics

Blackmail emails, where people will often send emails claiming to have some kind of embarrassing or compromising information on you. It is best not to give in but rather to report it to the right authorities.

Imposter websites: you may be following a tip from a friend or a link from an email, but it could lead you to a fake website. People have become masters in copying website designs and making them look like an authentic company. Keep an eye on the URL bar, and the security icon. If it is an HTTP and not an HTTPS then you need to think twice about the website you are working on. Make 100% sure you have the right URL in your browser, especially when working with cryptocurrency and money matters.

Fake apps on your mobile: scammers love tricking investors into downloading fake apps on Google Play or the Apple App Store. Although fake apps are removed, it doesn't mean damage cannot be done. It is known that a couple of thousand users have already downloaded a whole load of fake crypto apps. If you are an Android user, be extra careful. Check the logo, check the reviews, and check the name of the app for any subtle kind of misspellings. If something doesn't feel right to you, then play it safe and do not download the app.

Apart from blackmail, scammers try to send emails that look a whole lot like the cryptocurrency company. They like to add a sense of urgency, to make you act quickly before you think. Whenever you receive an important email, check the email address, check the links, and if it has anything to do with your account, visit the official website directly, and perhaps even contact them directly. Even if they install a sense of urgency, remember that most companies are professional, and would not expect you to drop everything and pay attention to them. Scammers, however, do.

Two Common Cryptocurrency Scams

Now the scams listed above can be both within the crypto world and in just everyday online work and scams. Here are the two crypto scams which you need to watch out for and directly avoid:

- New cryptocurrencies that have tons of hidden fees. Just like scammers in the real world, many frauds in crypto try to catch you with so many fine prints within contracts when you buy. And most of the time, people don't understand what is going on within a smart contract. So to avoid this kind of scam with any kind of cryptocurrency that you are interested in, purchase a small amount first, such as just $1 worth, and sell it afterward close to the same price. You will then be able to notice the massive resale fees that might be linked with the crypto that you are using.
- Sometimes people might even try and sell you cryptocurrencies that you cannot even resell. Hackers will write into the smart contract that their crypto can only be sold once and never again reselling, and then start by buying some of the cryptos themselves. Investors soon join the game, but their horror may realize that they simply cannot resell. A good example would be

to check out the Squid cryptocurrency, obviously riding on the popular trend of the South Korean's show "Squid Game," but having no actual link to the show. The best way to avoid a scam like this is simply sticking to the top 50 or top 100 of digital cryptocurrencies.

The Dark Side of Social Media

Social media is one of the best platforms for scammers to manipulate the market, send bad info, and even trick you into following the wrong links. Social media is not the platform you should use for solid and verified information, because you do not know or understand who is behind the screen.

Even if it is from a fan-favorite celebrity. They have even been hacked and messages are sent on their accounts leading people to pay cryptocurrency or simply accidentally install a virus because a celebrity had recommended it.

Hackers and scammers love using social media to spread misinformation and cause chaos in the markets too. Whether it is the pump and dump schemes, or making people pull out from crypto as quickly as possible.

Even if it is not a scammer directly posting, remember that everyone believes they are an expert online and will say just about anything to get famous. The problem is, very few people put in the work and the time to verify their facts, and you can guess what disaster that can bring to the table.

So here are some tips when working on social media:

- Do not use it as your source of information when it comes to investing
- Do not follow links provided by social media platforms, rather visit the website directly using your search engine
- Do not make any hasty decisions based on what is said on social media, verify first then make your decision
- Be very cautious of anyone who approaches you first on social media apps with their advice. I can promise you most of them do not have good intentions
- Just do your research on everything! It can take about 5 minutes sometimes to route out a scam. All it takes is a little Googling. Remember this, people become very verbal and public when they have been scammed online. And if scammers approach you, there is a huge chance you're not the first one they have tricked either.

Security Hacks for Your Computer

So this part of the chapter is to help prepare you against hackers and cybercrime where you do not necessarily have to open the door for them. Rather they try and hack you, and it is quite easy to do if you do not have your security measures in place. Remember, if you own crypto, you are your bank vault. Wouldn't you want to make the extra effort to make sure your bank vault security is up to date?

- Remember to keep the amount of personal information you share as limited as possible. Make sure they never have your home address, and be very careful of what you post on social media. Even keeping in mind the backgrounds and what information is on display there. I had to shake my head a couple of times as I saw the information my friends put online about themselves publicly. Not only could I track them down with just a name, but I could also find sensitive information.
- Remember to keep as many privacy settings online. There is a saying that if something is for free online, like a social media app, it means then that you are not the customer but the product. Marketers love to buy information about you, and so do hackers. But there are ways to control how much information is shared online, especially on Facebook. But keep in

mind, most companies make it difficult to find because they want your personal information.

- Safe browsing is key. Just like you won't want to walk through dark alleyways at night in the shady parts of your city, the same can be said about where you explore online. Cybercriminals focus on making content that will bait you, oftentimes called clickbait. All it takes is entering the wrong link for them to install a virus on your computer. So stick to the safe side online, have an antivirus control the links you enter, and just avoid giving hackers even a chance.

- Be very careful what you download onto your computer. Cybercriminals love making you download malware in the shape of apps or programs. These programs' primary goal is to steal information. So do not download files or software from websites you do not know or trust.

- When choosing passwords, choose long, strong, and complicated passwords. People love choosing easy passwords that they will remember, but do keep in mind easy passwords to remember are also easy passwords to guess. If it gets too complicated for you, then consider using password manager software, and you only then have to remember one very complicated password to access all your other complex passwords.

- Whenever you make purchases online, be sure to do them at secure sites. This is because you will be providing information such as your bank account or credit card—or in cryptocurrency, your private key—which is exactly what cybercriminals want. So be sure the URL is padlocked and the HTTPS (as the S does stand for secure).

- Also, as much as it is a thrill to meet people online, be very careful who you talk to and what information you want to provide. Keep in mind that people can hide who they are online, and fake social media profiles are the best ways for them to pick your pockets while becoming supposed friends.

- Your computer, cell phone, and any other device that has a connection to the internet should have an antivirus program. You also need to make completely sure that the antivirus program is completely up to date. Remember that hackers keep developing new viruses, and the antivirus needs to keep up, that means constant updates on your computer as well.

VPN

Apart from an antivirus, I would recommend that people also get a virtual private network (VPN). Why? Well, a VPN protects your information by hiding your IP address as well as encrypting any data that comes through secure networks. It is one of the best ways to hide your online identity, allowing you to work with cryptocurrency securely and anonymously.

Be sure, however, not to use free VPN services. Free VPN services sell your data or would even run ads on your computer which could have viruses to make up for their business costs. So as much as it may feel like a pain it is best to get a paid VPN.

The biggest problem with online security is the fact that most people cannot see the threat. The problem is, when it comes to online safety, the threat could be from anywhere in the world. As long as someone had the knowledge and connection to the internet.

So it is high time people ramp up their safety when it comes to meddling in the digital world, especially if you want to start participating in crypto. Cryptocurrency is quite an anonymous world, full of cloak and shadow. So when you want to work with it, why not bring your cloak with you? It will be in the shape of a VPN, antivirus, and doing your research before making any hasty decisions.

With that being said, it is time to look into the toolbox of what an investor needs to work with cryptocurrency and even consider investing. After all, you want to be able to store the tokens safely, and you want to use platforms that make it user-friendly.

Chapter 8: Digital Wallets, Exchanges, Brokers

Now, you are just at the beginning of your journey to investing in crypto. What do you need? Well, you want to know where to go obviously, and you also want to know where you can store what you buy. So, you may want to consider the following facts before choosing all the different platforms you would like to work on.

Digital Wallets

We all take our wallets when we go to the store. Otherwise, how could we buy anything? In some countries, a person can even carry a wallet on an app in their phone, scanning it to make necessary payments.

Considering that cryptocurrency is purely digital, you will not be able to store it in a physical wallet. A digital currency needs a digital wallet. But there are quite a few to choose from, and it is recommended to have more than one wallet.

Digital wallets for cryptocurrencies are normally called blockchain wallets, and you can use them to store your Ether, Bitcoin, or any other cryptocurrencies you have invested in. A blockchain wallet can also allow you to convert currencies back into your local currency.

How Do Blockchain Wallets work?

Well, electronic wallets store your cryptocurrencies and perhaps other digital assets such as NFTs. Depending on the wallet you get also depends on the type of cryptocurrencies you can store, as not every wallet can store every single crypto out there.

Most of the time, creating an e-wallet (electronic or digital) wallet is completely free, and you can set everything up online. Again, be very wise with the password you choose, and you can access your wallet either through logging into the Blockchain website, or even using a mobile application.

Online and Offline Wallets

There are also other electronic wallets which you can use. A blockchain wallet is an online wallet, as you can only access it online. But there are other online wallets. They are generally easier to work with, especially when moving different cryptocurrencies. But they are also a higher security risk. It means that it is far more likely that someone can hack and steal your cryptos.

An offline wallet is a wallet that you can store offline on your computer. It is far more secure and is generally recommended to store any sort of cryptocurrencies that you hope to keep for the long term. For example, if you would like to store Cardano, believing that it will go really big in two to four years.

It is recommended to have both an offline and an online wallet. You use your online wallet for any transfers and moving your cryptocurrency quickly, but it is best not to store all your cryptocurrencies in your online wallet. This is where your offline wallet will come in handy.

It is much like a shop where people keep petty cash for change in the front where people pay, but they store the larger amounts of money in the bank vault or safely hidden in the back of the shop. This is kinda how an online and offline wallet works.

Other Facts You Should Know About Crypto Wallets

Technically, very technically, crypto wallets do not store your crypto. Your cryptocurrency will always be on the blockchain itself. But you can only access the blockchain safely with the use of a private key. This is where the glass box analogy of blockchain comes in perfectly. The key that you have is proof of ownership which in turn will give you the chance to perform transactions. But if you were to lose your private key, you will lose any chance and access to that money. There are no resets of private keys or passwords when it comes to blockchain. It is why you store your private keys in wallets to make sure they cannot get lost.

Cryptocurrency Exchanges

If you are inexperienced or would like to make use of a good platform to start investing in crypto, then I would recommend you take a look at some of the cryptocurrency exchange platforms out there online. Why? Because they have built-in software dedicated to helping keep your money safe as well as helping you earn money.

Crypto exchanges are one of the most important tools investors tend to use when making transactions, and it is the most popular place where people want to buy or sell their cryptocurrencies.

Remember, cryptocurrency exchanges are centralized exchange platforms. It means there is a middleman involved to perform all the different transactions, and you will be trusting this middleman to help handle the assets. So yes, it partially works like a bank. If you are only interested in crypto for anonymity, then there are decentralized exchanges you can work on, but they are far less popular, and far harder to work with. So as a beginner, it may be best for you to work on a centralized platform, especially if you would want to learn from others and have a lot less work cut out for you.

The Differences Between Exchanges That Are Centralized and Decentralized

Centralized exchanges can be used to convert any fiat currency you are working with into cryptocurrency, or change your cryptocurrency into a fiat currency. You could also trade between different cryptos, such as exchange Ether for Bitcoin, Bitcoin for Ripple, etc.

Decentralized exchanges thoroughly cut out the middle man, and is generally a peer-to-peer exchange. All the services are done through smart contracts or other software, but no one ever has full control of the platform. It is, however, significantly less popular, but it has the potential of competing against centralized exchanges. It all just depends on what people want to see achieved in the future.

Key Points About Centralized Exchanges

There are always new centralized exchanges being made all the time, but not all of them are very successful, and not all of them are safe. Whether or not a cryptocurrency exchange platform is a good fit depends on how many people use it, and the security on the platform. Hackers love targeting exchanges, just look up Mt.Gox to understand why it is so important to make sure the exchange you choose focuses on security.

Top Cryptocurrency Exchanges

Currently the top crypto exchange platforms for the year 2022, here are some of the platforms you can check out and use for yourself if you want to:

- Coinbase - Online wallet is available along with strong security and charts as well as indicators to work with. But the user does not have control of the wallet keys, and you can choose a whole wide variety of different altcoins.
- Cash App - Great for beginners, has a wallet, works a lot like Venmo, and you can even withdraw Bitcoin. It is incredibly user-friendly. Unfortunately, it only supports Bitcoin and has withdrawal limits.

- Bisq - A decentralized exchange platform with about 15 different options of payment. The trading volume is quite low as well as the speed at which the transactions are taking place. So not a good choice if you would like to trade regularly.
- Binance - A lot of cryptocurrencies are available with lower fees and advanced charting. However, Binance cannot run in the US, and the Binance.US has fewer options for trading than the international version.

Cryptocurrency exchanges are ideal for people who do not necessarily want to trade in enormous amounts either. But if you would like some extra assistance, especially while learning how to trade in crypto, then it might be wise to check the online cryptocurrency brokers out there.

Cryptocurrency Brokers

What is a broker? Well, they are also middlemen, watching the trends and making trades on your behalf. When you want to buy stocks from companies, you normally need to use a broker. Imagine how awkward it would be if you had to walk into a business with a hundred dollars wanting to buy a stock with no idea of where to go. Brokers tend to work in between and can make it a little easier for people starting in cryptocurrency.

Using a broker means you have higher security as well as liquidity. What does that mean? Well, brokers often have a variety of different tools that you can use, including many technical analysis tools. What does that mean? It's tools that can allow you to pick up the trends and in which direction a cryptocurrency is going at that point and time. You can place automatic strategies and even help with risk, such as automatically pulling out of the market if the price goes too low.

Brokers also have tighter security, as well as offer a certain level of protection for your funds if a hack were to occur. Brokers focus on security at a higher level than exchanges.

But brokers are also known to charge higher fees, and using them means you might not be able to make traders 24/7. It does mean that if the market were to swing in a different direction, say on the weekend, your hands might be tied as the broker makes all the buying and selling for you.

So What Should I Use?

That is entirely up to you and what your goals are. Brokers and exchanges each suit a different type of client. If you are working with larger amounts of money, then I suggest trying out a broker. If you work with smaller amounts of money, then go with an exchange platform as it is more practical this way.

Either way, your next step would be to learn how to read charts to make 100% sure you can understand as well as apply any kind of trading strategy that you learn when investing with crypto. You don't want to be walking into crypto blindly, either. What if I told you there was a way to practice real-life trading and investing without paying a cent?

Paper Trading

Just like people learn how to fly first in simulators, there is a way to learn how to trade, read charts and predict trends without spending a single penny. And the beauty of it all is the fact that technology has come so far, it looks close to the real deal.

I introduce to you my best friend, paper trading. It is the best way for you to learn about buying and selling crypto without risking any of your money.

What exactly is paper trading? Well, in the olden days, people would practice trading with a piece of paper and keeping an eye on the live market. I can imagine a few hand cramps there from all the writing as they had to keep track of the 'trades' they were making, working out how much they made or lost during a trade.

Nowadays, there are many brokers or even crypto exchange platforms that offer paper trade accounts for you to use and practice in. Not only can you learn how to use that specific platform well, but you can also teach yourself the various ways how to trade before taking any risks at all.

There are many real-life simulators that would give you the chance to see and understand how your decisions and strategies would go in the live market as if they have been performed.

What are the advantages of paper trading?

- You can trade without any risk involved. This is ideal if you are just beginning to trade, and want to learn all the ropes without having to lose your money at the same time. Here, you can test out the strategies that you have learned, and see what works best for you and what doesn't.
- The simulator/demo accounts are a very close imitation of a real trading account. It means you can get used to the online trading accounts, and make the rookie mistakes on a platform meant for practice. It is important, however, to place the money that you realistically have in such an account, and not to work with insanely large amounts of money.

And what is the other side of paper trading?

- Well, because trading removes the risks, you won't encounter emotional obstacles because people tend to very easily get emotional when working with money, and do not think you will be the exception. It means that if you were to lose money on a demo account, you won't take it so seriously, and the decisions you make then versus when you are working with real money could be affected because of it.

- Information on the data is sometimes delayed for about 15-20 minutes so that the data on the live market cannot be used by competitors. Other simulators display fake data, and therefore it means not to fully follow the data provided on the demo when switching over to a real account.
- Sometimes trading on a demo does not consider all the costs either. So leave room for transaction fees etc which may be included in live trading but not paper trading.

But I will end this off by saying that using paper trading will bring many more advantages to your doorstep than simply trying to go off on it alone. Every single living person who wants to excel at something needs to practice first. A writer needs to practice writing. A soccer player needs to practice kicking the ball around and sending it to other players. An artist needs to practice painting or drawing.

A trader needs to practice trading, and an investor can practice investing. But you will find time and again that most people just take their chance and start in the real field. But who do you think will have more success?

Someone who has never run a marathon before decides to race, or someone who has put in the time and effort to practice and exercise before entering the race? So if you say that someone who has practiced paper trading you are correct.

Chapter 9: Crypto Mining

Now unless you are really into solving puzzles and working hard on your computer—plus being able to afford expensive equipment or hire equipment—crypto mining is simply another aspect of cryptocurrency that you need to be aware of. Anyone interested in joining mining can with the right tools and knowledge, even you, but right now, we're are just going to take a brief look as to why crypto mining is so important as well as understanding why there is an environmental impact with Bitcoin, and also why Ethereum is making changes in their system.

What Is Mining?

Cryptocurrency mining is the method used to verify any transactions as well as bring in new crypto tokens, such as Bitcoin, into circulation for people to use.

Crypto mining is known to be quite costly, but doesn't necessarily reward you for all the hard work, yet it has a great appeal for a great many people because miners do receive rewards when working. This is because of the entrepreneurial focus for many people, as much as the California gold prospectors had in the year 1849. And if you have the technological ability, why not take a swing at it?

For example, being rewarded with Bitcoin is a great incentive for many people to participate in the mining and monitoring of Bitcoin transactions to make sure they are completely valid. And because people are partaking in the mining from all across the globe in the running of Bitcoin, it allows for the decentralized network.

Understanding the Mining Process

Every single transaction is recorded into the distributed ledger called a blockchain. When each transaction occurs, specifically with Bitcoin, the transaction is processed and sent to one of the miners to be verified.

For a miner to verify a transaction, their computer needs to use proof of work (POW) where it is making a couple of billion transactions within a second. The moment the mathematical problem is solved, then the transaction is confirmed, verified, and added onto the blockchain. The miner and their computer who managed to solve the problem normally get rewarded with a new Bitcoin.

However, the more miners who start working on a specific cryptocurrency, the fewer Bitcoins are released over that specific period. This is known as Bitcoin halving, as the whole idea of Bitcoin and Bitcoin mining is to be achieved over a specific period.

Now, considering the value of Bitcoin, it is no wonder that people want to actively participate in mining, but it often requires the purchasing or hiring of special machines designed to run and mine cryptocurrencies. Here is where the economical issue comes in.

These machines take a lot of energy. And I mean, a lot.

The problem with cryptocurrency mining is that there are thousands of computers consuming energy, and because they are making a lot of heat, they also need to be cooled down. And each computer has a different way of using energy and cooling, which overall can take up to 121.36 terawatts each year.

This is more than what Google, Facebook, Apple, and Microsoft combined use in a year.

And for miners to compete against others, they will continue to increase their computing powers. It is one of the biggest reasons why China put a halt on Bitcoin and specifically Bitcoin mining due to the massive energy consumption that worked against China's goal to become carbon neutral by 2060. But this caused miners to move their operations and business to other countries that still rely a lot on fossil fuel, such as the US.

But the climatic impact that Bitcoin is having is dire and should be taken into consideration as the world is starting to feel the impact of the climate.

What Exactly Is Involved in Cryptocurrency Mining?

But how exactly does someone become a crypto miner? Well, crypto mining resembles the mining that takes place in actual mines when people are out searching for gold. But instead of digging in deep tunnels, people solve complex mathematical problems.

And the rewarding factor is once you have learned how everything works—it takes some time and effort to get a handle on mining—and once everything is set up, you can simply leave it and allow a source of passive income to pour in.

Now that it is heavily appealing to many people across the globe, especially in a struggling economy, it's no wonder that the idea of mining is so popular.

You will need three main components in mining:

- The digital wallet
- The mining software
- The mining hardware

You will need the wallet to gain the crypto tokens, the software, which is free to download and use depending on your operating system, and the hardware. The hardware is perhaps the most expensive to set up, and items just like the graphic cards could cost around $15,000.

There are alternatives, where you can take part in a mining pool where a group of miners shares all their computing power to mine a cryptocurrency. You will want to join a mining pool that is mining the crypto you would like.

Understanding Proof of Stake

Considering the climatic impact, many altcoins are not ignoring this problem that has been created by proof of work, the mathematical software that causes the major energy problems for mining. So many of them have decided to use proof of stake (POS) instead of proof of work.

Proof of stake allows owners of crypto to stake coins and create their kind of validator nodes. When you stake your coins, they are locked up, and you have to unstake them when you want to trade with them.

When you perform a transaction, the proof of stake protocol will again choose a node (computer - miner) to verify the block of information, and they check to make sure the information on the blockchain is completely valid.

If the person performing the transaction provides faulty information, they are then at risk of losing their staked holdings.

When miners work on proof of stake, they also have some of their crypto staked. However, the smaller your stake amount is, the decreased likelihood there is of you being chosen to validate the transactions and thus receive a reward.

Differences Between Proof of Stake and Proof of Work?

The main difference is the amount of energy that is used by a significant amount. Proof of work has a requirement that miners have to solve these huge puzzles. Proof of stake focuses on choosing a random person/computer to validate the information without having to solve a puzzle, it removes the major element that is sucking so much electricity.

It is far more likely that we will see the adoption of proof of stake in the crypto world to adopt the more eco-friendly version of the mining as well as making transactions and paying with digital money.

Chapter 10: NFTs

NFTs are taking the world by storm. Although they had arisen in 2014, they have recently captured the world's attention, and it is important for someone working with cryptocurrency to know about it. After all, apart from mining and trading, it is good to know all the options you have on making money on this platform, and this is specifically focused on the artists. If you have a creative streak in you or know somebody that does, then this might be another exciting opportunity for them.

But even if you don't have a creative streak in you, there are several ways you can make money with NFTs, and despite the intimidating name, NFTs are an easy idea to understand. It just needs to be explained correctly.

Most people have been left with many question marks around NFTs. It just exploded and has now become the next big thing in the digital world, but it somewhat doesn't altogether seem to make a lot of sense. What exactly is an NFT anyhow?

NFT Basics

NFT stands for Non-fungible token. For some reason, this makes me think of an old burger with a piece of cheese. Now that is entirely incorrect, and still leaves everyone in the dark, so let me explain a little more.

Non-fungible means that it is unique and irreplaceable. So if you think of fungible, it is likely that the device you are using to read this is fungible, as you can have more than one copy of it. A cryptocurrency is fungible. You can sell one Bitcoin, and buy a Bitcoin identical to the one you sold the very next day.

Non-fungible works more like a one-of-a-kind trading card. There is only one, and if you trade one trading card for another, you will find they will always be completely different.

So How Do NFTs Work Then?

So evidently it means that every last NFT is unique, and new, and cannot be found anywhere else? Technically yes. Taking a look at NFTs, they are generally a part of Ethereum's blockchain, and Ethereum as you well know is a cryptocurrency. But they also can support NFTs and store other kinds of information other than their Ether coin.

NFTs are the original version of a digital file. It could be digital artwork. It could be a digital music file. It could be a video. It can even be something as simple as a tweet, but NFT is currently most popular in the realm of digital art collecting.

Many artists and art collectors are hoping that NFTs can become an evolved and digitized form of collecting. An example would be someone paying over $390,000 for a 50-second video clip designed by Grimes.

But the thing is, NFTs are digital folders. And many digital folders can indeed be copied. This means although you can buy the authentic, original folder as well as the rights of using it in whichever way you please, it doesn't mean that people cannot access the same artwork, video clip, or music for free on another site. I mean, it's the internet. What are you supposed to expect?

However, only one person can truly own the original. And this is why NFTs are indeed so popular. I suppose it works a whole lot like a status symbol. People can flex and show off that they own the original picture, the original artwork, etc. I could go on and on and on.

So What Exactly Can I Do With NFTs?

It depends on two factors. You either approach the NFT as the artist or you are the one buying the NFTs.

If you are an artist, then well done, you have found yourself another great platform in which to sell your work, as well as have the chance of making big bucks with it. NFTs also enable you to earn a percentage every time someone sells your NFT. The best thing, it is automated, and the more popular your item becomes the more money you can start to earn from it, and the royalties you will be receiving.

If you are the buyer or collector, you will be able to support artists you very specifically like, and have the rights to use the NFT in any way you so deem fit. You could even buy artworks with hopes that the value of whatever you bought does go up and you can indeed sell it for a profit.

So Who Would Buy NFTs?

Well, this is where it gets just a little tricky. NFTs do indeed work like trading cards, and you are selling to a market that deems that NFT is the future of fine art collecting, and they would like to be ahead of the curve.

Other people treat NFTs very much like Pokémon cards. It is where normal people can access it, but it is just the market for the super-rich.

Can I Start Selling NFTs?

Yes! You certainly can, but

And I hate to say there is a but...

BUT you will have to have built up for yourself a social media platform or built up an audience who would want to buy your artwork ideas. And that is probably the part every person overlooks when bringing up the idea of NFTs.

Unless you are already a celebrity, you will have to work to gain the attention of the audience and convince them the item you are selling is worth the price. Do I believe that anyone has that capability and goals? Sure! But it does take a lot of hard work, a great idea, and certainly, a lot of luck to get that far.

Are There NFT Scammers as Well?

Unfortunately yes, there are also scammers lurking around the NFTs. Many of them are simply trying to get into your digital wallet and steal the NFTs that you own, but others write some insane code hidden in an NFT.

For example, some hackers send "gifts" of NFT to people, but once a person clicks on it, it will wipe out their balance. Many similar scams are running on NFT like this one, and it would be wise to practice caution. Again, you first need to open the door for the hacker by accepting the gift, so just don't go around accepting gifts from strangers, and this sounds an awful lot like telling children not to accept candy from strangers. It will get you quite far in life.

Wherever you go online, and whenever there is money involved. You will always be finding people trying to scam you, and because NFTs much like crypto are unregulated, people tend to be able to get away with a lot more. So caution always needs to be practiced, and keep an eye on what is said within the communities, people who fall for crypto traps tend to speak up about it very quickly. Same can be said about NFTs.

Understanding NFT and the Environment

And yes, because we are working on blockchain again, unfortunately, the environment needs to be brought up...again.

But it is not something we can simply ignore when it comes to cryptocurrencies. I am not saying crypto should be shut down, but I do believe more effort and work needs to be put in to find eco-friendly ways of applying the technologies on the different blockchains before even considering to go any further with any kind of technology to do with blockchain.

When you create an NFT, it is called a minting process. This process, as you may have guessed or might not have, takes a whole lot of energy. The bigger the NFT, the more energy, and you are charged for gas fees.

Again, the use of excess energy harms the environment and could be the reason for NFT's downfall in the future. NFT leaves a heavy carbon footprint. It is difficult to have an exact estimate of how much energy and carbon emissions NFT are leaving behind, but it is said to be a very big chunk.

Unless of course, the artists and main users of NFTs push for a more eco-friendly approach. Ethereum itself is starting to take on the POS network, and considering that NFTs run mostly on Ethereum, it means that overall, NFTs are starting to head towards a greener future.

But the future of where NFTs are headed is just as uncertain as cryptocurrency itself. All I know is that you need to keep an eye on all this in the oncoming decade. Everything that will be happening in the next ten years will be a great reflection of the future of NFTs and cryptocurrency. For example, it is possible that

Bitcoin might not survive, and Ethereum could take the throne. Or, it may be possible that a thoroughly new cryptocurrency strides forward to the throne, kicking everything out of place and leaving people perplexed for the next couple of years to come. It's up to you to watch out, and keep an eye on the trends.

Don't follow every trend, but it is wise to be aware of them, especially in regards to the market. Knowledge and research are the best things you can do for yourself. Even an extra five to thirty minutes really can make all the difference in the world as to the decisions you want to make.

So, regardless of whether or not it is NFT or cryptocurrency, put the time in. The less you know about something, the greater the risk. You want to earn money, but to do so, you want to reduce as much risk as possible, especially when working online and especially when working with an already volatile form of money.

Conclusion

And now we have finally reached the end of the book, and may I be the first to tell you well done! You have gone through quite a journey, and now you understand the basic foundational necessities to get started with cryptocurrency. But before you go, I just want to go into a little recap and leave a few parting tips to take with you on your investment journey.

First of all, you understand what money is now. You know how it works, how it runs, and why currencies are different to each other. Money is essential to running the modern day economies, and a person can pretty much get almost nowhere without money. People slave away hours of the day to earn money, and as society advances to a more digital life, it is no surprise that we are heading towards digital and electronic payments. Many countries' goals are to try and aim for a cashless society. Naturally, certain places are closer than others.

But with banks comes a lot of history, and a lot of that history is not positive. There is still a lot of anger and mistrust that runs with the governments and any centralized financial companies. And the truth is, most of the economy is run and dependent on a few big companies. Which means, they have a lot of control over the way things go.

Next, we have the rise of cryptocurrency, when Satoshi Nakamoto launched Bitcoin in the year 2009. We learn it is a physical form of money run on blockchain, and people can make payments on a global basis with faster speeds as well as decreased fees. As Bitcoin started to become more popular, we saw a rise of many other different altcoins, which are cryptocurrencies designed after Bitcoin.

Naturally, there are way too many cryptocurrencies to list them all, considering there are over 16,0000, so the top altcoins were listed. And if you are interested in investing in crypto, I highly recommend that you stick with the more established cryptos until you gain enough knowledge, wisdom, and experience to still steer clear from the new and risky cryptos that are more likely gonna strike you with a loss.

But due to the instability, people had come up with a different kind of cryptocurrency called a stablecoin. And they stuck. Stablecoins have their value tethered to another commodity, generally a fiat currency like the US dollar, allowing people to benefit from both making cryptocurrency transactions while seeing higher levels of stability. But the companies that run stablecoins are centralized, and are under constant pressure to be audited and monitored by third-parties, as they are competing with completely transparent cryptocurrencies. One of the primary reasons why people use crypto is due to its decentralized nature, which is why they as centralized digital coins have a lot more to prove.

But when working online and with digital money, it is naturally going to attract the thieves and robbers of the online world, and cryptocurrency is notoriously filled with frauds, hackers, and scammers. So you need to practice extra caution when working online, following through on the hacks provided and spend the necessary time verifying any information given to you. Be equally paranoid and suspicious, and if anything does feel off to you, don't hesitate to wait or decline whatever is being offered. Most of the time, it is the scammers and hackers that need you to open the door first for them before they can get in and wreak havoc. So why not take the necessary steps to make sure you never open the door for them?

Apart from safety, there are also a variety of tools you'll need to learn to work with to invest in crypto. There are digital wallets, for example, and practical reasons as to why you should have an offline and an online wallet. You also need to decide whether or not you want to use a cryptocurrency exchange platform, or a broker platform. Most of these platforms also provide you with paper trading, which is perfect for practicing your trading and investing skills before actually entering the live market. I can guarantee you most experts and traders would recommend you to start practicing first, as it can teach you so much which cannot necessarily be explained in a tutorial.

Leading on, you have learned now about cryptocurrency mining, and why it is another opportunity to earn some money passively, once you have set everything up. It is, however, problematic if the blockchain runs on POW, as it consumes a lot of energy which in turn harms the environment. Many crypto blockchains have started adopting POS that dramatically reduces the amount of energy used, but still allows you to reap benefits from mining.

Alongside mining, NFTs have also sprung into action, mostly working on the Ethereum blockchain, and have taken the world by a storm. NFT is a great way for artists to make money, but even if you are not an artist, you can still earn money by buying and renting NFTs that are popular, or selling NFTs for a profit once the value of an item rises. However, NFTs do take a more sales-like approach in comparison to cryptocurrency's trading approach, and a different skill set will have to be learned to profit from NFTs. NFTs also share the same eco damaging issue alongside blockchain, but solutions are being designed to help solve this problem.

So all in all, there are both benefits and cons to trading in crypto. The more information that you gather for yourself, the better. The best tips I can give you is to always do your research before investing, and to follow the number one trading rule no matter where you are in life, and what you want to achieve:

- Never invest money in crypto which you cannot afford to lose

Why is that? Because cryptocurrency is still incredibly risky. It might not deter you from investing, but your whole goal is to earn more money. You do not want to leave trading worse off than you were before, and it is the number one mistake so many people make when they start investing.

Don't be that person. Rather, have patience, and grow the money. Do not use your retirement funds, and do not apply for a loan. Understand that trading and investing, even with crypto, is a patience game. The quick rich schemes are commonly scams.

Don't be afraid of cryptocurrency either though. Practice caution and safety but allow yourself to take the occasional but sensible risks. If there is something you do not understand, just dig a little deeper. Even if it is simply Googling the larger terminology—large words that make no sense when strung together. I have to admit I do it all the time, which in turn, allows me to explain matters and ideas which although thought to be complex, is just stuffed with so much jargon that it sounds fancy.

And remember to enjoy it! You cannot make a journey and decision such as trading without feeling the thrill and rush of having a victory. Some days you'll win and some days you'll lose. But you want to know a little secret? The biggest secret is to get back up, take a step back if you need to calm down, and learn from your mistakes.

I believe most success comes only after a string of failures, even when it comes to matters of crypto.

References

Boom, D. V. (2022, January 13). *NFTs explained: Why people spends millions of dollars on JPEGs*. CNET. https://www.cnet.com/news/nfts-explained-why-people-spends-millions-of-dollars-on-jpegs/

Cho, R. (2021, September 20). *Bitcoin's Impacts on Climate and the Environment*. State of the Planet. https://news.climate.columbia.edu/2021/09/20/bitcoins-impacts-on-climate-and-the-environment/

Coinbase. (2022). *Crypto basics - What is a crypto wallet?* Www.coinbase.com. https://www.coinbase.com/learn/crypto-basics/what-is-a-crypto-wallet

Conway, L. (2021, November 8). *Best Crypto Exchanges*. Investopedia. https://www.investopedia.com/best-crypto-exchanges-5071855

Daly, L. (2021a, September 24). *What Is Proof of Stake (PoS) in Crypto?* The Motley Fool. https://www.fool.com/investing/stock-market/market-sectors/financials/cryptocurrency-stocks/proof-of-stake/

Daly, L. (2021b, September 24). *What Is Proof of Stake (PoS) in Crypto?* The Motley Fool.

https://www.fool.com/investing/stock-market/market-sectors/financials/cryptocurrency-stocks/proof-of-stake/

DeMatteo, M. (2021a, November 12). *Crypto Scams Are on the Rise — Here's How Investors Can Protect Their Coins.* Time. https://time.com/nextadvisor/investing/cryptocurrency/common-crypto-scams/

DeMatteo, M. (2021b, December 8). *There Are Thousands of Different Altcoins. Here's Why Crypto Investors Should Pass on Most of Them.* Time. https://time.com/nextadvisor/investing/cryptocurrency/altcoins/#:~:text=%E2%80%9CAltcoin%E2%80%9D%20refers%20to%20any%20type

EBR, E. (2021, November 1). *Future of Blockchain: How Will It Revolutionize The World In 2022 & Beyond!* The European Business Review. https://www.europeanbusinessreview.com/future-of-blockchain-how-will-it-revolutionize-the-world-in-2022-beyond/

Elena. (2021, May 14). *How to trade cryptocurrency: key points and tips.* StormGain_crypto. https://medium.com/stormgain-crypto/how-to-trade-cryptocurrency-key-points-and-tips-c70a50896981

ET Spotlight. (2022, February 5). Watch: Amit Singhania, Partner, Shardul Amarchand Mangaldas. *The Economic Times.* https://economictimes.indiatimes.com/watch-

amit-singhania-partner-shardul-amarchand-
mangaldas/articleshow/89365264.cms

ETX Capital. (2022). *The Top 3 Cryptocurrency
Trading Tips And Strategies | ETX Capital.*
Www.etxcapital.com.
https://www.etxcapital.com/en/education/lear
n-cryptocurrencies/cryptocurrency-trading-
tips-and-strategies

Federal Trade Commission. (2021, April 21). *What to
know about cryptocurrency and scams.*
Consumer Information.
https://www.consumer.ftc.gov/articles/what-
know-about-cryptocurrency-and-scams

Frankenfield, J. (2020). *What Is a Blockchain Wallet?*
Investopedia.
https://www.investopedia.com/terms/b/block
chain-wallet.asp

Frankenfield, J. (2021a, February 18). *Bitcoin.*
Investopedia.
https://www.investopedia.com/terms/b/bitcoi
n.asp

Frankenfield, J. (2021b, April 26). *Altcoin.*
Investopedia.
https://www.investopedia.com/terms/a/altcoi
n.asp

Frankenfield, J. (2022, January 15). *Bitcoin
Exchange.* Investopedia.
https://www.investopedia.com/terms/b/bitcoi
n-exchange.asp

Friedberg Direct. (2022). *What is Paper Trading?
Pros and Cons Explained | Friedberg Direct.*
AvaTrade.

https://www.avatrade.ca/education/correct-trading-rules/paper-trading

Hayes, A. (2019). *Stablecoin*. Investopedia. https://www.investopedia.com/terms/s/stablecoin.asp

Kaspersky. (2019). *Top 10 Internet Safety Rules & What Not to Do Online*. Kaspersky; Kaspersky. https://usa.kaspersky.com/resource-center/preemptive-safety/top-10-internet-safety-rules-and-what-not-to-do-online

Kaspersky. (2021, January 13). *4 Common Cryptocurrency Scams and How to Avoid Them*. Www.kaspersky.com. https://www.kaspersky.com/resource-center/definitions/cryptocurrency-scams

Kaushik, V. (2021, November 15). *Stablecoins Explained- Types, Examples, Advantages and Investing Guide | Analytics Steps*. Www.analyticssteps.com. https://www.analyticssteps.com/blogs/stablecoins-explained-types-examples-advantages-and-investing-guide

Kenton, W. (2019). *Hyperinflation*. Investopedia. https://www.investopedia.com/terms/h/hyperinflation.asp

Khan, D. (2018, June 14). *3 Analogies That Explain How Blockchain Technology Works*. TransformationWorx. https://www.transformationworx.com/post/2018/06/07/3-analogies-that-explain-how-blockchain-technology-works

Liebkind, J. (2022, February 8). *Beware of These Five Bitcoin Scams.* Investopedia. https://www.investopedia.com/articles/forex/042315/beware-these-five-bitcoin-scams.asp

Muthyala, S. (2021, September 6). *10 Tips for Cryptocurrency Trading That All Investors Should Know.* Analytic Insight. https://www.analyticsinsight.net/10-tips-for-cryptocurrency-trading-that-all-investors-should-know/

N26. (2022, January 17). *The pros and cons of cryptocurrency: A guide for new investors.* N26.com; N26. https://n26.com/en-eu/blog/pros-and-cons-of-cryptocurrency

Nova, A. (2021, July 3). *Here's what cryptocurrencies will look like in 50 years according to experts.* CNBC. https://www.cnbc.com/2021/07/03/what-cryptocurrencies-will-look-like-in-50-years.html

October 19 2021, T. (2021, October 19). *Why you must be cautious while investing in cryptocurrencies.* Business Daily. https://www.businessdailyafrica.com/bd/lifestyle/personal-finance/cautious-investing-cryptocurrencies-3587600

Outlook. (2022, February 10). *Here Is Why Cryptocurrencies Are So Volatile.* Https://Www.outlookindia.com/. https://www.outlookindia.com/website/story/business-news-here-is-why-are-cryptocurrencies-so-volatile/398988

Qiu, J. (2021, April 20). *What Are NFTs, And What is Their Environmental Impact?* Earth.org. https://earth.org/nfts-environmental-impact/

Reiff, N. (2021a, August 25). *How to Get Established as a Cryptocurrency Miner.* Investopedia. https://www.investopedia.com/news/how-get-established-cryptocurrency-miner/

Reiff, N. (2021b, August 26). *What's the environmental impact of cryptocurrency?* Investopedia. https://www.investopedia.com/tech/whats-environmental-impact-cryptocurrency/

Satsuk, P. (2020, November 25). *Cryptocurrency Exchange vs Broker: What Should You Know Before Choosing?* Soft-FX. https://www.soft-fx.com/blog/cryptocurrency-exchange-vs-broker/

Scott, N. (2016, July 28). *Nearly Half of All Americans Don't Trust the Banks.* Living Wealth. https://livingwealth.com/nearly-half-americans-dont-trust-banks/

Shead, S. (2021, December 17). *Bitcoin "may not last that much longer," academic warns.* CNBC. https://www.cnbc.com/2021/12/17/bitcoin-may-not-last-that-much-longer-academic-warns.html

Sinha, D. (2021, August 31). *Investors, Top Stablecoins Set To Replace Bitcoin In Future!* Analytics Insight. https://www.analyticsinsight.net/investors-top-stablecoins-set-to-replace-bitcoin-in-future/

www.ingramcontent.com/pod-product-compliance
Lightning Source LLC
Chambersburg PA
CBHW021433180326
41458CB00001B/248